I HAD A LITTLE NUT TREE

Nursery Rhymes are themselves: they are basic. They have here returned to base. In our modern world they appear in many forms. Those that are meant for the home and that add elaborate displays in the accompaniment, serve but to show up how resistant are these tough, enduring little entities of his own folklore that are every child's heritage, to attempts upon their real nature. These here offered belong where they begin, on mother's knee, and find unadorned their simplest essential.

Because for the intimacy of shared performance, English nursery rhymes lend themselves most faithfully to accompaniment upon a keyboard instrument, and a piano is in many homes, these accompaniments are devised for any parent of little musical skill and a child upon their lap. To this extent it is a musician's book, of one who first knew rhymes in this way and has gone on loving them so long as life is.

It is not sufficiently realized that as the tunes are meant for singing, there are many which it is inappropriate necessarily to try and reproduce upon an instrument. They simply need underpinning. Once the tune is known and sung, hand positions established, piano fingers move by easy step, no more demanded than to keep things going.

This collection, of which this book forms a part, is founded on the rhymes included in those gracious classics *The Baby's Opera* and *The Baby's Bouquet* and their antecedents, the rhymes and tunes edited and the accompaniments brought up to date in our own time. May it bring all who grow from these roots to the joyful truth 'in my end is my beginning'.

ELIZABETH POSTON

PART THREE OF THE BABY'S SONG BOOK

I Had a Little
Nut Tree

ELIZABETH POSTON

ILLUSTRATIONS BY
WILLIAM STOBBS

THE BODLEY HEAD
LONDON SYDNEY
TORONTO

because of
CLEMENTINE
for dear Elizabeth Craggs
PHILIP AND
ANTHEA

Musical settings © Elizabeth Poston 1971
Illustrations © William Stobbs 1971
ISBN 0 370 01528 2
Printed in Great Britain for
The Bodley Head Ltd
9 Bow Street, London WC2E 7AL
by William Clowes & Sons Ltd, Beccles
Music engraved by Lowe & Brydone (Printers) Ltd
First published 1971

CONTENTS

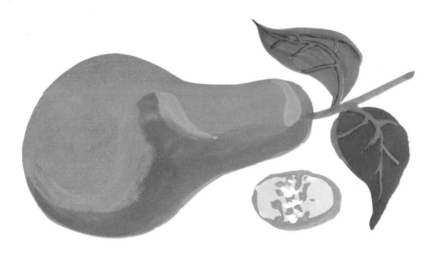

I HAD A LITTLE NUT TREE

I had a lit-tle nut tree, No-thing would it bear

But a sil-ver nut-meg And a gold-en pear; The

King of Spain's daugh-ter Came to vi-sit me, And

all — for the sake Of my lit-tle nut tree.

I had a little nut tree,
  Nothing would it bear
But a silver nutmeg
  And a golden pear;
The King of Spain's daughter
  Came to visit me,
And all for the sake
  Of my little nut tree.

7

HOT-CROSS BUNS!

Hot-cross Buns! Hot-cross Buns! One a pen-ny, two a pen-ny,

Hot-cross Buns! Hot-cross Buns! Hot-cross Buns!

If your daugh-ters do not like them, Give them to your sons.

If you have no daugh-ters, If you have no daugh-ters,

If you have no daugh - ters,_ Give them to your sons; But if you have - n't a - ny of these pret - ty lit - tle elves, Then_ you must eat_ them_ all your - selves.

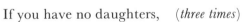

Hot-cross Buns!
Hot-cross Buns!
One a penny, two a penny,
Hot-cross Buns!

Hot-cross Buns!
Hot-cross Buns!
If your daughters do not like them,
Give them to your sons.

If you have no daughters,   (*three times*)
Give them to your sons;
But if you haven't any of these pretty little elves,
Then you must eat them all yourselves.

9

BAA, BAA, BLACK SHEEP

Baa, baa, black sheep, Have you a-ny wool? Yes, sir,

yes, sir, Three bags full; One for the mas-ter, And

one for the dame, And one for the lit-tle boy Who lives down the lane.

Baa, baa, black sheep,
   Have you any wool?
Yes, sir, yes, sir,
   Three bags full;
One for the master,
   And one for the dame,
And one for the little boy
   Who lives down the lane.

AIKEN DRUM

1. There_ was a man lived in the moon, lived

in the moon, lived in the moon, There_ was a man lived

in the moon, And his name was Ai-ken Drum; And he

played up-on a la - dle, a la - dle, a la - dle, And he

played up-on a la - dle, And his name was Ai-ken Drum.

1　There was a man lived in the moon,
　lived in the moon, lived in the moon,
　There was a man lived in the moon,
　And his name was Aiken Drum;
　And he played upon a ladle,
　a ladle, a ladle,
　And he played upon a ladle,
　And his name was Aiken Drum.

2　And his hat was made of good cream cheese,
　And his name, &c.

3　And his coat was made of good roast beef,
　And his name, &c.

4　And his buttons were made of penny loaves,
　And his name, &c.

5　His waistcoat was made of crust of pies,
　And his name, &c.

6　His breeches were made of haggis bags,
　And his name, &c.

7　There was a man in another town,
　And his name was Willy Wood;
　And he played upon a razor,
　And his name was Willy Wood.

8　And he ate up all the good cream cheese,
　And his name, &c.

9　And he ate up all the good roast beef,
　And his name, &c.

10　And he ate up all the penny loaves,
　And his name, &c.

11　And he ate up all the good pie crust,
　And his name, &c.

12　But he choked upon the haggis bags,
　And that ended Willy Wood.

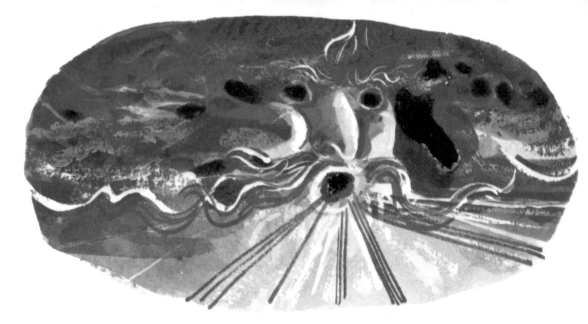

THE NORTH WIND

The north wind doth blow, — And we shall have snow, And what will poor Ro - bin do then, poor thing? He'll sit in a barn — And keep him - self warm, And

hide his head un - der his wing, poor thing.

The north wind doth blow,
And we shall have snow,
And what will poor Robin do then, poor thing?
He'll sit in a barn
And keep himself warm,
And hide his head under his wing, poor thing.

RING-A-RING
O' ROSES

Ring - a - ring o' ro - ses, A po - cket full of po - sies, A - tish - oo! A - tish - oo! We all fall down.

Ring-a-ring o' roses,
A pocket full of posies,
A-tishoo! A-tishoo!
We all fall down.

DERRIÈRE DE CHEZ MON PÈRE

MY FATHER'S APPLE TREE

Acc. © Elizabeth Poston 1971

1. Der - rièr' de chez mon pè - re, Lan la, lan - di - gue da,
1. *Back there, be-hind my fa - ther's, Lon la, lon - dig - ga da,*

Der - rièr' de chez mon pè - re, Lan la, lan - di - gue da,
Back there, be-hind my fa - ther's, Lon la, lon - dig - ga da,

Un pom - mier il y a, Lan - di - gue - di - gue lan lir',
There is an ap - ple tree, Lon - dig - ga - dig - ga lon lir,

Un pom-mier il y a, Lan - di -gue-di -gue lan lir'.
There is an ap-ple tree, Lon - dig - ga-dig - ga lon lir.

1 Derrière de chez mon père,
  Lan la, landigue da,
  Derrière de chez mon père,
  Lan la, landigue da,
  Un pommier il y a,
  Landiguedigue lan lire,
  Un pommier il y a,
  Landiguedigue lan lire.

2 Il y a autant de pommes,
  Lan la, landigue da,
  Il y a autant de pommes,
  Lan la, landigue da,
  Que de feuilles il y a,
  Landiguedigue lan lire,
  Que de feuilles il y a,
  Landiguedigue lan lire.

3 Mad'leine d'mande à son père,
  Lan la, landigue da,
  Mad'leine d'mande à son père,
  Lan la, landigue da,
  Quand on les cueillera,
  Landiguedigue lan lire,
  Quand on les cueillera,
  Landiguedigue lan lire.

4 A la Saint-Jean, ma fille,
  Lan la, landigue da,
  A la Saint-Jean, ma fille,
  Lan la, landigue da,
  Quand la saison sera,
  Landiguedigue lan lire,
  Quand la saison sera,
  Landiguedigue lan lire.

1 Back there, behind my father's,
  Lon la, londigga da,
  Back there, behind my father's,
  Lon la, londigga da,
  There is an apple tree,
  Londiggadigga lon lir,
  There is an apple tree,
  Londiggadigga lon lir.

2 It is as full of apples,
  Lon la, londigga da,
  It is as full of apples,
  Lon la, londigga da,
  As it is full of leaves,
  Londiggadigga lon lir,
  As it is full of leaves,
  Londiggadigga lon lir.

3 Mad'leine she asks her father,
  Lon la, londigga da,
  Mad'leine she asks her father,
  Lon la, londigga da,
  When picking time will be,
  Londiggadigga lon lir,
  When picking time will be,
  Londiggadigga lon lir.

4 Saint-John, midsummer, daughter,
  Lon la, londigga da,
  Saint-John, midsummer, daughter,
  Lon la, londigga da,
  That's when they picked will be,
  Londiggadigga lon lir,
  That's when they picked will be,
  Londiggadigga lon lir.

from Edmée Arma: *Entrez dans la Danse.*
Henry Lemoine et Cie, Paris. By permission.

PUSSY CAT, PUSSY CAT, WHERE HAVE YOU BEEN?

Pus - sy cat, pus - sy cat, where have you been?

I've been to Lon - don to look at the queen.

Pus - sy cat, pus - sy cat, what did you there?

I caught a lit - tle mouse un - der her chair.

Pussy cat, pussy cat, where have you been?
I've been to London to look at the queen.
Pussy cat, pussy cat, what did you there?
I caught a little mouse under her chair.

OLD KING COLE

1. Old King Cole was a mer-ry old__ soul, And a mer-ry old soul was he; He__ called for his pipe, And he called for his bowl, And he called for his fid - dlers__ three.

Ev - 'ry__ fid - dler he had a fine__ fid-dle, And a ve - ry fine_ fid-dle had_ he:

Verses 1 and 2 repeat three times
Verse 3 repeat four times

Twee-dle dee, twee-dle dee, twee-dle
Twee-dle dee, twee-dle dee, twee-dle
O there's none so__ rare As__

dee, twee-dle dee,
dee, twee-dle dee,
can com - pare
With King Cole and his fid - dlers_ three.

2 Old King Cole
  Was a merry old soul,
  And a merry old soul was he;
  He called for his pipe,
  And he called for his bowl,
  And he called for his harpers three.
  Ev'ry harper he had a fine harp,
  And a very fine harp had he:
  Twang-a-twang, twang-a-twang,
    twang-a-twang, twang-a-twang,
  Tweedle dee, tweedle dee,
    tweedle dee, tweedle dee,
  O there's none so rare
  As can compare
  With King Cole and his fiddlers three.

3 Old King Cole
  Was a merry old soul,
  And a merry old soul was he;
  He called for his pipe,
  And he called for his bowl,
  And he called for his pipers three.
  Ev'ry piper he had a fine pipe,
  And a very fine pipe had he:
  Tootle too, tootle too, tootle too, tootle too,
  Twang-a-twang, twang-a-twang,
    twang-a-twang, twang-a-twang,
  Tweedle dee, tweedle dee,
    tweedle dee, tweedle dee,
  O there's none so rare
  As can compare
  With King Cole and his fiddlers three.

OH, WHAT HAVE YOU GOT
FOR DINNER, MRS BOND?

1. Oh, ___ what have you got for din-ner, Mis-sis Bond? There's beef ___ in the lar-der, and ducks ___ in the pond; Dil-ly, dil-ly,

dil - ly, dil - ly, come__ to be killed, For

you__ must be stuffed and my cus - to - mers filled.

1   Oh, what have you got for dinner, Mrs Bond?
    There's beef in the larder, and ducks in the pond;
    Dilly, dilly, dilly, dilly, come to be killed,
    For you must be stuffed and my customers filled.

2   John Ostler, go fetch me a duckling or two,
    Ma'am, says John Ostler, I'll try what I can do;
    Cry, Dilly, dilly, dilly, dilly, come to be killed,
    For you must be stuffed and my customers filled.

3   I have been to the ducks that swim in the pond,
    But I found they won't come to be killed, Mrs Bond;
    I cried, Dilly, dilly, dilly, dilly, come to be killed,
    For you must be stuffed and my customers filled.

4   Mrs Bond she went down to the pond in a rage,
    With plenty of onions and plenty of sage;
    She cried, Come, little wag-tails, come to be killed,
    For you must be stuffed and my customers filled.

E ARRIVATO L'AMBASCIATORE

HERE'S THE AMBASSADOR, HE'S ARRIVING

E ar-ri va - to l'am-ba-scia-to - re di suoi
Here's the am-bas - sa-dor, he's ar - riv - ing from his

mon - ti e dal - le val - li; E ar - ri - va - to l'am-ba-scia-
moun-tains and by the val - leys; O the am - bas - sa-dor he's ar-

1	E arrivato l'ambasciatore	1	Here's the ambassador, he's arriving

1   E arrivato l'ambasciatore
      di suoi monti e dalle valli;
      E arrivato l'ambasciatore.
      a-io-là, io-là, io-là.

2   Che cosa vuole, l'ambasciatore?
      di suoi monti e dalle valli;
      Che cosa vuole, l'ambasciatore?
      a-io-là, io-là, io-là.

3   Noi vogliamo una bimba bella
      di suoi monti e dalle valli;
      Noi vogliamo una bimba bella.
      a-io-là, io-là, io-là.

4   E come la vestirete?

5   Le vestiremo di pelle d'oca.

6   Ora no, non siam' contenti.

7   La vestiremo con un vestito
      di brillianti.

8   Ora si, che siam' contenti.

9   Ecco gli sposi che vanno
      a marito,
      Con due gento anelli in dito;
      Cento di qua, cento di là,
      Ecco gli sposi che sene vàn'.

10   Se ne vanno a Santa Croce,
      Ecco gli sposi che schiaccian'
      le noce;
      E ne schiaccian' due a tre,
      Ecco gli sposi che vanno
      a seder'.

1   Here's the ambassador, he's arriving
      from his mountains and by the valleys;
      O the ambassador he's arriving.
      a-io-là, io-là, io-là.

2   What are Excellency's wishes?
      from his mountains and by the valleys;
      What are his Excellency's wishes?
      a-io-là, io-là, io-là.

3   A fair girl is what we're asking
      from his mountains and by the valleys;
      A fair girl is what we're asking.
      a-io-là, io-là, io-là.

4   Now we've brought her, how shall
      we dress her?

5   We will dress her all in a goose skin.

6   That won't do; we won't accept it.

7   Then, we'll give her a dress of diamonds.

8   That is fitting; we're quite content now.

9   Here are the bridegrooms, who come
      a-singing,
      Two attendants the gold rings bringing;
      A hundred here, and a hundred there,
      Then to church they're off, they'll soon
      be there.

10   It's to Holy Cross they're going,
      Cracking nuts, that's what they're doing;
      They'll be cracking them round the town,
      And now the bridegrooms all sit down.

MERRILY DANCE
THE QUAKER'S WIFE

Mer - ri - ly dance the Qua - ker's wife,

Mer - ri - ly dance the Qua - ker; Mer - ri - ly dance the

Qua - ker's wife, Mer - ri - ly dance the Qua - ker.

She was a semp - stress all her life,

He was an un - der - tak - er; Mer - ri - ly dance — the

Qua - ker's wife, Mer - ri - ly dance the Qua - ker.

Merrily dance the Quaker's wife,
　Merrily dance the Quaker;
Merrily dance the Quaker's wife,
　Merrily dance the Quaker.
She was a sempstress all her life,
　He was an undertaker;
Merrily dance the Quaker's wife,
　Merrily dance the Quaker.

LAVENDER'S BLUE

1. La - ven - der's blue, did - dle did - dle,

La - ven - der's green; When I am

king, did - dle did - dle, You shall be queen.

1   Lavender's blue, diddle diddle,
       Lavender's green;
    When I am king, diddle diddle,
       You shall be queen.

2   Call up your men, diddle diddle,
       Set them to work;
    Some to the plough, diddle diddle,
       Some to the cart.

3   Some to make hay, diddle diddle,
       Some to cut corn;
    While you and I, diddle diddle,
       Keep ourselves warm.

JACK AND JILL

Jack and Jill went up the hill To

fetch a pail of wa - ter;

Jack fell down and broke his crown, And

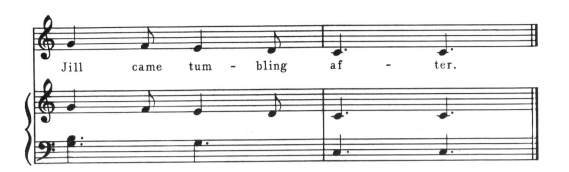

Jill came tum - bling af - ter.

Jack and Jill went up the hill
   To fetch a pail of water;
Jack fell down and broke his crown,
   And Jill came tumbling after.

WIDEWIDEWENN
BIDDY BIDDY BURKEY

Wi - de - wi - de - wen - ne heisst mei - ne Trut -
Bid - dy Bid - dy Bur - key's the name of my

hen - ne, Kann - nicht - ruhn heisst mein Huhn,
tur - key, Dash - ing Dick he's my chick,

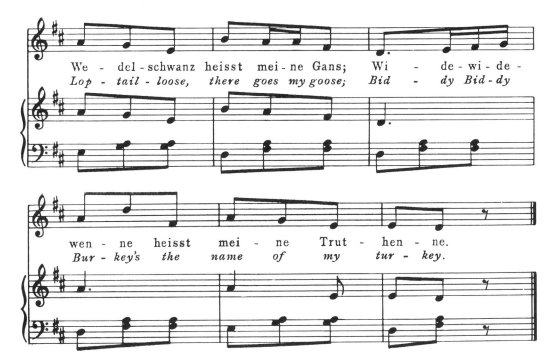

We - del - schwanz heisst mei - ne Gans; Wi - de - wi - de -
Lop - tail - loose, there goes my goose; Bid - dy Bid - dy

wen - ne heisst mei - ne Trut - hen - ne.
Bur - key's the name of my tur - key.

Widewidewenne heisst meine Trut-henne,
Kann-nicht-ruhn heisst mein Huhn,
Wedelschwanz heisst meine Gans;
Widewidewenne heisst meine Trut-henne.

Widewidewenne heisst meine Trut-henne,
Entequent heisst meine Ent',
Sammetmatz heisst meine Katz;
Widewidewenne heisst meine Trut-henne.

Widewidewenne heisst meine Trut-henne,
Schwarz und weiss heisst meine Geiss,
Schmortöpflein heisst mein Schwein;
Widewidewenne heisst meine Trut-henne.

1 Biddy Biddy Burkey's the name of my turkey,
Dashing Dick he's my chick,
Loptail-loose, there goes my goose;
Biddy Biddy Burkey's the name of my turkey.

2 Biddy Biddy Burkey's the name of my turkey,
Quickquackquuck she's my duck,
Pusspitpat, there goes my cat;
Biddy Biddy Burkey's the name of my turkey.

3 Biddy Biddy Burkey's the name of my turkey,
White'n-black-coat he's my goat,
Tuck-pot-tig, there goes my pig;
Biddy Biddy Burkey's the name of my turkey.

THE LITTLE
COCK SPARROW

1. A little cock sparrow sat on a green tree, And he chirrupped, he chirrupped, so merry was he; A little cock sparrow sat on a green tree, And he chirrupped, he chirrupped, so merry was he; He chirrupped, he chirrupped, he chirrupped, he chirrupped, He

chir-rupped, he chir-rupped, he chir-rupped, he chir-rupped, A lit-tle cock spar-row sat

on a green tree, And he chir-rupped, he chir-rupped, so mer-ry was he.

1 A little cock sparrow sat on a green tree,   *(twice)*
    And he chirrupped, he chirrupped, so merry was he;
    He chirrupped, he chirrupped, he chirrupped, he chirrupped,
    He chirrupped, he chirrupped, he chirrupped, he chirrupped,
    A little cock sparrow sat on a green tree,
    And he chirrupped, he chirrupped, so merry was he.

2 A naughty boy came with his wee bow and arrow,   *(twice)*
    Says he, I will shoot this little cock sparrow;
    I will shoot, I will shoot, I will shoot, I will shoot,
    I will shoot, I will shoot, I will shoot, I will shoot,
    A naughty boy came with his wee bow and arrow,
    Says he, I will shoot this little cock sparrow.

3 His body will make me a nice little stew,   *(twice)*
    And his giblets will make me a little pie too;
    His giblets, his giblets, his giblets, his giblets,
    His giblets, his giblets, his giblets, his giblets,
    His body will make me a nice little stew,
    His giblets will make me a little pie too.

4 Oh, no, said the sparrow, I won't make a stew,   *(twice)*
    So he fluttered his wings and away he flew;
    He fluttered, he fluttered, he fluttered, he fluttered,
    He fluttered, he fluttered, he fluttered, he fluttered,
    Oh, no, said the sparrow, I won't make a stew,
    So he fluttered his wings and away he flew.

TOM, THE PIPER'S SON

Tom, Tom, the pi-per's son Stole a ___ pig and a-way he run; The pig was eat And Tom was beat, And Tom went ___ roar - ing down the street.

Tom, Tom, the piper's son
Stole a pig and away he run;
    The pig was eat
     And Tom was beat,
And Tom went roaring down the street.

THE OLD WOMAN
AND THE PEDLAR

1 There was a lit-tle wo-man, As I've heard tell,
She went to mar-ket, Her eggs for to sell,
Fol, lol, did-dle did-dle dol; She went to mar-ket All on a mar-ket day, And she fell a-sleep Up-on the king's high-way. Fol de rol de lol lol lol lol lol, Fol, lol, did-dle did-dle dol.

There was a little woman,
As I've heard tell,
  Fol, lol, diddle diddle dol ;
She went to market,
Her eggs for to sell;
  Fol, lol, diddle diddle dol ;
She went to market
All on a market day,
And she fell asleep
Upon the king's highway.
  Fol de rol de lol lol lol lol lol,
  Fol, lol, diddle diddle dol.

There came by a pedlar,
His name was Stout,
  Fol, lol, diddle diddle dol ;
He cut her petticoats
All round about;
  Fol, lol, diddle diddle dol ;
He cut her petticoats
Up to the knees,
Which made the little woman
To shiver and sneeze.
  Fol de rol de lol lol lol lol lol,
  Fol, lol, diddle diddle dol.

3 When the little woman
Began to awake,
  Fol, lol, diddle diddle dol ;
She began to shiver,
And she began to shake;
  Fol, lol, diddle diddle dol ;
She began to shake,
And she began to cry,
Lawk-a-mercy on me!
This is none of I.
  Fol de rol de lol lol lol lol lol,
  Fol, lol, diddle diddle dol.

4 If this be I,
As I hope it be,
  Fol, lol, diddle diddle dol ;
I've a little dog at home
And he knows me;
  Fol, lol, diddle diddle dol ;
If it be I,
He will wag his little tail,
If it be not I,
He will bark and rail.
  Fol de rol de lol lol lol lol lol,
  Fol, lol, diddle diddle dol.

5 Home went the little woman
All in the dark,
  Fol, lol, diddle diddle dol ;
Up starts the little dog
And he began to bark;
  Fol, lol, diddle diddle dol ;
He began to bark,
And she began to cry,
Lawk-a-mercy on me!
This is none of I.
  Fol de rol de lol lol lol lol lol,
  Fol, lol, diddle diddle dol.

LITTLE MISS MUFFET

Lit - tle Miss Muf - fet Sat on a tuf - fet,

Eat - ing her curds and whey; _____ There

came a big spi - der Who sat down be - side her, And

fright - ened Miss Muf - fet   a - way. _____

Little Miss Muffet
Sat on a tuffet,
Eating her curds and whey;
There came a big spider
Who sat down beside her,
And frightened Miss Muffet away.

PRETTY LITTLE HORSES

1. Hush you bye, Don't you cry, Go to sleep-y, lit-tle ba - by; When you wake, You shall have cake, And drive those pret-ty lit-tle hor - ses.

1 Hush you bye,
Don't you cry,
Go to sleepy, little baby;
When you wake,
You shall have cake,
And drive those pretty little horses.

2 Hush you bye,
Don't you cry,
Go to sleepy, little baby;
Blacks and bays,
Dapples and grays,
And coach and six-a little horses.

SAN SERENÍ DEL MONTE
SAINT SERENÍ OF THE MOUNTAIN

1. San Se - re - ní del mon - te, San Se - re -
1. Saint Se - re - ní of the moun - tain, court - eous and

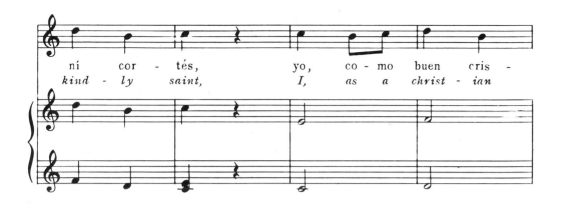

1	San Serení del monte, San Serení cortés, yo, como buen cristiano, yo me arrodillaré.	1	Saint Serení of the mountain, courteous and kindly saint, I, as a christian child, I'll kneel me down to pray.
2	San Serení del monte, San Serení cortés, yo, como buen cristiano, yo me sentaré.	2	Saint Serení of the mountain, courteous and kindly saint, I, as a christian child, I'll sit me down from play.
3	San Serení del monte, San Serení cortés, yo, como buen cristiano, yo me echaré.	3	Saint Serení of the mountain, courteous and kindly saint, I, as a christian child, I'll stretch me down to lay.
4	San Serení del monte, San Serení cortés, yo, como buen cristiano, yo me levantaré.	4	Saint Serení of the mountain, courteous and kindly saint, I, as a christian child, I'll get me up at day.

INDEX OF FIRST LINES